DOWTCHA BOY!

***Morty McCarthy** is a native of Cork.*
He is the drummer in well-known Cork band
the Sultans of Ping FC. He now lives in Stockholm
where he teaches Swedes to speak English
with a Cork accent.

DOWTCHA BOY!

An Anthology of Cork Slang

Morty McCarthy

Published in 2010 by Morty McCarthy

First published in Ireland in 2004 by The Collins Press

British Library Cataloguing in Publication data.

Printed in Ireland by ColourBooks Ltd.

This book is printed on paper manufactured with the greatest possible care for the environment.

Typesetting: Joanna Andreasson
Typeface: Berthold Akzidenz Grotesk & Acropolis

Illustrations: Fergus Keane
Editing: Michael Moynihan

ISBN: 978-0-9567070-0-0

www.dowtchaboy.com

In memory of my grandparents,
Breda and Jimmy
Kathleen and Morty

I would like to thank my family, especially Emma, Nina, Kilian, Derek Higgins, the staff at Folkuniversitetet in Stockholm, Långholmen FC members, Pakie Aherne, Kieran Burke at the Cork City Library and most of all, the people of Cork for their help with this book.

CONTENTS

INTRODUCTION

Welcome to the world of Cork – a world where pigs' feet and sheep's stomachs are part of the staple diet. People play all sorts of strange card games. The train station is built on a bend. Adults buy their reading glasses in novelty shops. People drink rasa and Tanora. The population is forever 136,000. All sorts of unusual feast days are celebrated (Bonfire Night, Corpus Christi, Women's Little Christmas). A place where traditional sports such as rings, draghunting and road bowling are still hugely popular. In short, Cork is a unique city. Every place is unique, of course. This book, however, is a celebration of Cork's uniqueness and more particularly a celebration of its language.

Cork is the second city of Ireland, situated near the south coast. It's a city that has never suffered from 'second city syndrome' because its citizens firmly believe it to be 'De Real Capital'. It is built on rolling hills and the accent rises and falls in imitation of the landscape. There are a bewildering variety of accents within the city itself. Cork people love to talk and are extremely skilled in their use of language.

In a way, I have been writing this book all my life. Many of the words gathered are part of my own vocabulary. I picked up the new and unfamiliar words by simply listening to the people of Cork speak. You won't find a lot of these words in books. New words are constantly coming into our vocabulary, just as old ones disappear. So in a way this will always be an unfinished book. It's impossible to draw a line in the sand and say that all the words we use have been 'found'. I am certain that there are many words out there that have escaped my attention.

It is important to keep a record of our language. It tells us a lot about who we are. Cork is a city rich in character and deserves to be recorded as such.

One of the most remarkable things I discovered whilst writing this book was the large difference in the language used in various parts of the city. For example, almost everyone on the northside I spoke to knew what the term 'strawkhauling' meant whereas most southsiders looked at me blankly. On the other hand a word such as 'rcyc' would be common knowledge in Douglas, though relatively unknown in other parts. Many people in the more affluent areas of the city seem to be unaware that 'rasa' is a traditional Cork drink at Christmas.

Everyone has their own version of what Cork is.

With regard to the words themselves I have spelt them as they sound. There is a great deal of difference between the spoken and written language and I have tried to capture the feeling of the spoken word in Cork.

I hope you get as much enjoyment from reading this book as I did from writing it.

Up the rebels,
Morty

DE GRAMMAR OF IT ALL

Trying to find a structure to the way people speak in Cork is no easy task, especially since the spoken word is so different to the written word. Cork people have their own set of unwritten rules governing language which are not taught in school; these quirks are learnt from one another. Some of these irregularities have been passed down the generations, others disappear, new ones turn up. It is hard to find where things start and end. When, for example, did the word 'langer' start to be used in the city? Why do some words catch on while others disappear? It is very rare nowadays that you would hear the word 'latch' in use, whereas twenty years ago it was in common usage.

The use of language in Cork should, of course, be celebrated. It's one of the things that makes Corkonians different. As the drive towards globalisation continues, there is a pressure on the English language to also conform. People should instead celebrate the eccentricities in the use of language; these are often more interesting than standard English. Whilst writing this book certain irregularities in Cork speech cropped up time and time again. Many of these quirks are not limited to Cork but are also found in other parts of the English-speaking world.

WORD MISCONCEPTIONS
Most people in Cork seem to think that they go to the 'pantomine' at Christmas when in fact they are going to the *pantomime*!

Corkonians sharpen their pencils with a 'pero' when it should be called a *parer*. Most Cork people head out for a drink or five to celebrate 'Stephenses Day' when actually it's *Stephen's Day*. Strangely, when we put the word saint in front of Stephen the mistake usually disappears (St Stephen's Day). Lots of people like going for a walk along a 'clift' when the word is *cliff*.

OUT OF FASHION WORDS

The use of 'ye' when addressing more than one person is common in Cork. This is a very old form of the plural 'you' that has fallen out of use in most other parts of the world where English is spoken. Corkonians listen to the 'wireless' and take a 'sup' from a 'tin' of Fanta when in most other places, they listen to the *radio* and take a *sip* from a *can* of Fanta. Numerous other examples exist of these out of fashion words – e.g., bunburger, ware, delph, doing a line, nicks, togs, scauld, tell-tale tattler, donkey's years.

PRONUNCIATION

Cork's most famous mispronunciation is undoubtedly the 'th' sound. In fact most Cork people leave out the 'h' entirely so that the word 'thing' for example sounds like 'ting', 'that' sounds like 'dat'.

This gives outsiders endless hours of amusement. How many times has someone asked you to say the number 'tirty tree'?

Maybe there is some bizarre link between Cork and the West

Indies? It's time to erect signs at the county bounds saying that 'h's' aren't welcome. Corkonians also have a tendency to drop the 't' from the end of a word when it turns up in expressions like 'wha' harm'.

Nicknames in the city often end in a 'y' sound, for instance, Deccy, Micky, Johnny, whereas in Dublin they often end in o – Decco, Anto, Micko, Johnno, etc.

The 'ah' sound at the end of many words seems unique to the city. Take these examples: Barracka, Buttera, Billa, Cha and Miah, foolah, snake-a, blackas. An 'a' is often substituted for 'on' in Cork speech – 'I'll se ya a Monday', for example.

Some of the mispronunciations are funny to an outsider: 'We saw a *filum* and it was *brillant',* as opposed to 'it was a brilliant film'. Bowling ('bowel-ing') is another classic word where Cork pronunciation is completely at odds with the rest of the world.

VERB FORMS

The most common verbs in the English language are to be, to have and to do. Cork people often use 'dudn't' instead of does-n't in the third person singular: 'He dudn't know anything 'bout it boy.' The word 'it' quite often disappears and becomes part of the verb. For example: ''twas a grand wedding', ''tis a lovely day', 'the weather forecast said 'twill be nice tomorrow', ''twon't matter at all'.

'Wadn't' – instead of wasn't – is still in common usage in the city: 'The match wadn't bad'. Past tenses of certain verbs can also be odd, to say the least. Many people use 'brang' as the past tense of bring when, in fact, it's 'brought: 'I brang the *Echo* home with me'. Other variations include: 'I'll be *kilt* (killed) when I get home because I *scrope* (scraped) my leg on a wall', 'He blemt (blamed) me for doing it'.

USE OF IRISH

It's heartening to see the influence the Irish language has on the way we speak, even though this is sometimes played down. Often we retain the word as it is, such as, 'we had great *craic* last night', 'he's a right *amadán*'. Sometimes we translate the words into English: 'He has no mass on that (*meas* – respect)'. Slang words such as '*beor*' (girl) come from the native language. Irish gives an extra language tool to work with. All languages have gaps where they lack a word that perfectly suits a certain meaning. Irish helps fill those gaps in spoken English.

YOU WHA'?

Some strange things also turn up in Cork speech. We say 'I will ya' when we mean no, and 'how bad' when something is good. Cork speech is peppered with the words 'la' and 'like'. Technically, such words are non-essential, but they are frequently used to add emphasis. 'Here you are la', 'it's over there la', 'I know what you mean like'. You could pass yourself off as a Corkman by simply using just 'la', 'like', 'will ya' and 'how bad' in every other sentence.

Cork people are never hungry, jealous or sound. It's more a

case of being 'hungry out', 'jealous out' and 'sound out'. Favourite adjectives seem to be 'fierce' and 'pure'. 'There was a fierce crowd in town last night' might indicate violence to a foreigner when it's actually only a comment on the numbers in town 'doing pana', so to speak. 'The crowd went pure mental out the Cross when Georgie got the winner' conveys the intensity of the crowd's reaction when celebrating a goal.

When trying to remember something we want to say, the expression 'wasiname' is often used as a conversation filler, giving us time to think about what we want to express.

The use of 'along' is another unusual one. Cork people use this preposition to indicate direction (which is consistent with its correct use), except in Cork it is used to finish our sentences instead of following it with an object, e.g., 'I'm going up along' means I'm going home. 'Going down along' usually means 'going into town'.

PURE CORK LIKE

GONE FISHIN'

BAYTUR: Huge fish
I caught a baytur of a bass last night down Church Bay.

BREAK/BREAKING: Fish, particularly mackerel, attacking sprats on the surface
The mackerel were breaking all over the place in Camden.

DAWK (1): To hook a fish in the body by accident
Dessie dawked a three pound pollack down the Old Head the other night.

GERMAN SPRAT: Type of fishing hook used for spinning
The Tackle Shop are selling six German sprats for five yoyos.

PUCK: To hook a fish in the body deliberately
I pucked two salmon down the Lee Fields yesterday.

STRAWKHAULING (1): Method used to catch fish illegally, usually salmon, using a line, a treble hook and a weight
There was a few fellas strawkhauling down on the Shakey Bridge.

TOIRNEENS/TOIRNEELS: Small minnows found in the Lough, amongst other places
Jimmy has a rake of toirneens at home in a Joyce's tin.

DE BOYS AND DE GIRLS

BAZZ: Female pubic hair
I'd bate the bazz off her, boy.

BEOR: Female
Check out the beor over there la.

BOXED: Pregnant
Jacinta's boxed again.

BRASSER: Prostitute/Loose woman
I saw a load of brassers down the docks.

BOODAWN: Erection
Look at the boodawn on him.

CHATS: Breasts
She has a fine pair of chats, God bless her.

DOLLYB'S: Girls
There were some fine dollyb's in Henry's at Sweat on Saturday.

FIFTY: When someone stands you up
I got a fifty last night from yer wan.

FINE STAB: Good-looking person
Shirley Buckley is a fine stab, isn't she?

FLAH (1): To have sex with
I flahed a fine thing from Dublin last night.

FLAH (2): Extremely good-looking person
Roisin Mullins is a flah.

FLAH BAG: Trollop/Loose woman
She's a right flah bag that one.

GET THE BULLET/GET BLOWN OUT: Get turned down
I got the bullet off Audrey when I asked her out.

GO AWAY WITH SOMEONE: To have a one-night stand
I went away with a wan I met at a party.

GOOSAH: Person surplus to requirements on a date
I'm not playing goosah for ya.

HANGING: Ugly
You can't go home with her, she's hanging.

JAG: Date
I have a jag with Alison tonight.

JAGGING: Going out with someone
I'm jagging at the moment.

LASHER: Extremely good-looking person
The new Miss Spiders is a bit of a lasher.

NOBBER: Sexual pervert
He's a bit of a nobber, that fella.

ON THE BOX: Having sexual intercourse
I was on the box last night.

OUL DOLL: Girlfriend
I'm going to the pictures tonight with the oul doll.

PICTURE NO SOUND: Not on talking terms
It's all a bit picture no sound with the missus at the moment.

SCRAPE: Sexually obliging female
She's a fine scrape, yer wan Sharon.

SHIFT/STALL: French kiss
I got a great shift off Debbie at the grads.

STEAMER: Homosexual
He's a steamer that fella.

TROT: Dance
Are you coming for a trot girl?

WEAK: The feeling when you fancy someone
I'm only weak for him.

WHERE WE SPORTED AND PLAYED

ALL A BAA: Card term meaning the stakes on the table are up for grabs. One of the players shouts this and attempts to grab the money. Can only be shouted once in an evening's card playing.

BANISH: To lose a ball in a game of street football or hurling by hitting it over a wall, into a house, etc
Keep the sliotar down so we don't banish it.

BENUIN: Card term meaning cheating
Watch him, he's benuin.

BLOOD AND BANDAGE: Name for Cork GAA teams which reflects the colours of the kit.
C'mon the blood and bandage.

BURN (1): To run rings around an opponent
That corner back is getting burned by Setanta.

DON: Old card game mainly played in Cork and Dublin
There's a game of don going on in the lounge.

DRAGHUNT: Cross country dog race where harriers follow a scent around a course. The winner is the first dog to complete the trail.
The harriers are having a draghunt out in Waterfall a Sunday.

FUNKY: Cowardly
He's one funky hurler, that fella.

HAUNTED: Lucky
The Barrs were haunted to beat the Glen in the Eucharistic match.

HAVE A CUT: Have a go
Joe Deane is going to have a cut off the sideline puck.

LEATHERA: Leather football
Did anyone bring a leathera with them?

NINER: Card game
Who's in for a game of niner?

SCORE: Game of bowls
There's a score on in Whitechurch today.

SKEETING: Sliding
We're going skeeting on the Lough.

SLOGGING (1): Street game of hurling or soccer involving two players
C'mon we have a game of slogging.

THREE GOALS IN: Street soccer game
Let's play three goals in – bags not in goal.

TOEDRIVE: To kick the ball with the front of your foot

No toedrives allowed in this game, lads.

UNDER THE INFLUENCE

BUSH DRINKING/BUSHIN': Drinking outdoors
We went bushin' down Canty's Field Friday night.

BUSH TAVERN: Name of the imaginary outdoor pub
We were in the bush tavern last night.

DRAG SOMEONE ON: To pay for someone's drinks when they have no money
Don't worry, I'll drag ya on boy.

GATT: Alcohol
Who is going up to Gally's for the gatt?

GATTING: Drinking alcohol
There was a massive crowd gatting down the college after the results came out.

GAWK UP: To get sick
I gawked up all over the bathroom last night when I got home.

GET THE GAWKS: To feel sick/About to be sick
I'm getting the gawks, open the window fast.

GREAT LIP: Fondness for the drink
Himself has great lip for the pints.

GREAT TACK: Great stuff
This new cider is great tack.

LANGERS/LANGERATED: Extremely drunk
I was langers last night at the wedding.

MAGALORIM: Drunk
We were all magalorim on the stag night.

MEDIUM: Half pint. The regular drink of a woman in times gone by in the snug of a pub
A pint of Beamish for meself and a medium for the missus.

MOMBOLISED: Very drunk
Johnny Shea was mombolised when I saw him last night up Shandon Street.

ON THE RAN-TAN: On a bender
We were on the ran-tan out in Blarney for the day.

ON THE TACK: Off the drink
I'm on the tack for the Holy Souls.

QUART: Pint
Are you coming for a quart later?

STEAMED TO THE GILLS: Drunk
We were steamed to the gills at the twenty-first the other night.

TINT: Small amount
Can I have a tint of red lemonade in the whiskey?

TWO L: Two litre of cider
They're selling two Ls for five euro down in Bradley's.

DESCRIBING THINGS

BAKE: Mess
You made a bake of that, ya langer.

BALMPOT/BALMER: Nutcase
That fella is a balmpot.

BERRIES (THE): Excellent
That filum we saw last night was the berries.

BIRDIE: Kiss
Give yer favourite aunt a birdie.

BRAZEN WALLOP: Saucy person
She's one brazen wallop, that one O'Leary.

C4: Cork upper-class accent equivalent to D4 in Dublin. Also refers to the group of people who speak with the accent.
Crosshaven will be full of C4's for the Ford Week.

CAFFLER: Troublemaker/Gurrier
He's a right caffler that fella.

CHATTY BOO: Whatchamacallit. Often used when a person can't remember the name of something.
You'll have to get a chatty boo to fix that.

COD A: Made up
That story is only cod a.

CRABBIT: Cute
Donie's small one is very crabbit, she'd buy and sell ya.

DAWFAKE: To counterfeit
He's after dawfaking an ID to get served.

DOONCHIE: Tiny
His new flat is doonchie, you couldn't swing a cat in it.

DROPPIN': Dying to go to the toilet
Stop the car as soon as, I'm droppin'.

FLAHED OUT: Exhausted
I'm flahed out from working too much.

FOOLAH: Eejit (Idiot)
He's a bit of a foolah.

GLIGEEN: Stupid individual
They're a right bunch of gligeens.

GOMEY: Slow in the head
He's a bit gomey, that fella.

GOVVY: Posh/Snobby
They're very govvy up in Montenotte.

GOWLMONGERING: Acting the fool/Messing
Stop yer gowlmongering or I'll keep ye in after school.

GUTTY: Rough
He's a pure gutty boy.

GUZZ EYE/SCOOT EYE: Squinty eye
He's got a bit of a guzz eye.

HACK: Laugh/Craic
Shur 'twas only a bit of hack.

HANDY DOCKET: Hard case. Used in an affectionate, playful way
You're one handy docket alright.

JOLTER: Laid back person
He's an oul jolter, isn't he?

KIDDY (THE): Excellent
The new album by the Franks is the kiddy.

KNOTTED/SKITTING: Laughing heartily
We were knotted at the pantomine last night.

LANGERLOAD: Large amount
There was a langerload of people in Sidetrax last night.

LIVELY MURPHY: Poacher
Some lively Murphy is after stealing a few chickens.

LU-LA: Spacer
They're a right couple of lu-las.

MOCKEY AH: Pretend/Not real
That was only a mockey ah fight they were having.

MOLLEY AH: Made up
That thing she said was only molley ah.

POXED: Lucky
I was poxed to pass my exams.

PULL A BOOTER: Leave immediately
Lads, I'm pulling a booter away off home.

ROYALLER: Great time
I'd say they're having a royaller out in Santa Ponsa.

SCOVE: Brisk walk
I'm going for a scove out Blarney way.

SHANDONS: Balls
Do you want a kick in the shandons?

SOOLACH: Dirty/Manky
Don't wash the ware in that water, it's soolach.

THE BULB OFF: The image of
Yer man is the bulb off Tom Selleck.

TOME: Grand/Sound
Let him in, he's tome.

WHAT PADDY CANTY CAUGHT OUT THE LOUGH: Nothing
Did you get anything off yer wan?
I got what Paddy Canty caught out the Lough, f-all.

WIRELESS: To have the same accent
We're all wireless these days.

WACKER SPEAK

APACHE: Joyrider
The law were chasing an apache up Opel Road.

ARE YOU CARRYING?: Have you a loan of some money?

ASS: The end of something that someone is eating.
I'm up the ass of your mars bar.

BE WIDE: Be vigilant
Be wide there, the shades are coming.

BULBS: Eyes
Check out the bulbs on yer man.

CLAIM: Challenge to a fight
I claim ya boy.

COT: Bed
I'm off to me cot, I'm flahed out.

DAWK (2): Punch
I got a dawk in the head outside Burgerland Friday night.

DOGHANDY: Very good fighter
He's doghandy that fella.

DOGWIDE: Extra vigilant / Wary
You'd want to be dogwide of him.

FEEK: To shag
I feeked a beor up Fitzgerald's Park yesterday evening.

FEEN: Boy
There was a rake of feens hanging around outside the chipper.

GALUN: Idiot
Yer man Byrne is some galun.

GAMMIN: Cork slang
Do you speak the gammin?

GATCH/GAUTCH/GAANCH: The way someone walks.
Different versions of this word are used around the city
Check out yer man's gatch there la.

GLUG: To spit
Someone is after glugging on your duffle coat.

GLUGGER: Spit
There is a big glugger on your back.

GO: One against one fight after school. Everyone stands
around watching and shouts go, go, go go go
There's a go on between Fitzy and Roy.

HALE: A drag off someone's cigarette
Gis a hale off that will ya boy.

HOBBLE: To steal
I hobbled a few cans in Donovan's.

HOP ON (1): Free for all fight
There was fierce hop on after the match.

HOP ON (2): To jump in and help a friend out in a fight
John was getting a beating so I hopped on for him.

KICKSHIT: Violent game of football with no rules
C'mon, we have a game of kickshit.

KNOCK: Thing
Hide the knock before the lawman sees it.

L.O.B.: Warning shout meaning look out boys
L.O.B. the shades are coming.

MOG: Fool
He's some mog, isn't he?

NODGE: Piece of hash
I'm after dropping the nodge in the grass.

ONE BULB: Garda motorbike
There was a one bulb 'round the estate last night.

PHANTOM: Special branch car
Be wide boys, there is a phantom parked over there keeping sketch on us.

PIGSTY: Police station
I spent the night in a pigsty.

QUARTER IRONS: Metal studs put on the soles of shoes to make a wacker seem even tougher
O'Brien is going to ban quarter irons in school.

REEF: To steal from someone
Someone is after reefing me pint.

SCATTER (1): Fight
There was a fierce scatter outside the pub.

SCONCE: Quick look
Have a sconce of that there la.

SCOOT ON: Move on quickly
I'm scooting on before the law come.

SHADES: Gardai
Leg it before the shades arrive.

SHOWERY: Cry of warning
Showery! There's a two bulb pulling in.

SLAPLESS: Poor fighter
That fella is slapless, he couldn't beat his way out of a paper bag.

SOLK: To steal
We solked a car down de Marsh de other night.

STALL ON/STALL THE BALL/STALL THE BEANS: Hold on
Stall the beans there now kid a second.

TULL: Troublemaker
There's always a couple of tulls hanging around by the shop.

TWO BULB: Garda squad car
Scoot on there boys, there is a two bulb on the way up along.

UP THE STEPS: Going to the courthouse
You'll be going up the steps if you're not careful.

WACKER: Cork corner boy/troublemaker
There's a rake of wackers hanging out by the Five Star.

WAX: To shin up a pole or pipe
I waxed up that pole no problem.

CORK CLASSICS

A NOBLE CALL: A singer's right to name the next singer at a party. This is an older English term still in common usage in the city
I have a noble call and since that call is mine,
I'll tell you what I'll do, I'll call on 'name'.

ACT THE LANGER: Do the fool
Don't be acting de langer now kid.

BACKER: To have someone on the back of your bike
Gis a backer down to the shop, will ya girl?

BAGS: To claim something as yours
I found the ball so I bags it.

BALLHOP: To wind up
I was only ballhopping ya kid.

BALM OUT: To lie out in the sun
We were balmed out down the beach in Garrettstown on Sunday.

BAZZER: Haircut
I must get a bazzer down in Frankie Ford's.

BONA: Bonfire
Someone solked all the tyres from our bona.

BOY: Used when addressing a male of any age
How are ya boy?

BREAK YOUR MELT: To frustrate/Try your patience
John's oul doll would break your melt.

BUTTY: Variation in pronunciation of the word buddy
This is me butty Damien.

CANCEL THAT: Change of plans after saying something.
The expression can be used in different ways.
A common example: *Cancel that – we'll have that.*

CHANEY EYE: False eye
Uncle Billy used to take out his chaney eye and play with it.

CONNISHURE: Gossip
She's an awful connishure that wan.

CONNISHURING: Gossiping
The connishuring that goes on at work is no one's business.

CRIBBIN': Whinging and moaning
Stop cribbin' and get on with it.

CROSSER: To have someone on the crossbar of your bike
Gis a crosser down to the village.

DAGENHAM YANK: Name given to Cork people who used to work in Ford's in Dagenham in East London.
One of their favourite sayings is: *It was tough in nam (i.e Dagenham) but even harder in the bush (Shepherd's Bush).*

DE PAPER: *The Examiner*
I read in de paper today that Jenning's is closing down.

DO THE DJ: DJ-ing
Who's doing the dj at the wedding on Saturday?

DOING PANA: Walking up and down Patrick Street spotting talent and chatting to people
There were some fine halves around when I was doing pana on Saturday.

DOTE: Lovely person
She's an oul dote, that one.

DOWN THE BANKS: To give out to
I'll give him down the banks when I catch him.

DOWTCHA BOY: Expression of praise which means well done
Dowtcha Davey Barry boy.

ECHO BOYS: Newspaper sellers in Cork
The Echo *Boys make a handy few extra bob selling the* RTE *Guide.*

FLAH (3): To take the piss
Ah you're flahing the situation now.

FOXER: Job where no tax is paid
I had a handy couple of foxers in the last few weeks.

FUNT: Kick
Go way before I give ya a funt up the ass.

GIRL: Used to address a female of any age
Are ya coming down de bingo, girl?

HOW BAD: An expression meaning good
I won a weekend for two in Galway – shur how bad.

LANGER (1): Penis
You should have seen the size of his langer, Concepta.

LANGER (2): Idiot
G'wan, ya langer ya.

LAPSI PA: Non-existent disease
That fella has a touch of the lapsi pas.

ME DAZA: Excellent
Two pints of rasa, I think you're me daza.

MEBS (1): Balls
I got some kick in the mebs playing soccer the other night.

NODEENAW: Indecisive person
She's some nodeenaw alright.

NORRIE: Someone from the northside
The place was crawling in norries.

OUL LAID/OUL MAN: Mother/Father
The oul laid is after grounding me for two weeks.

PIGEON: Pot for urinating in
Tell that nurse to bring the pigeon in to me as I can't get out of the bed.

PLANK: To hide
Plank the gatt before the oul man gets back.

PLAYER: Friend. Used in a greeting
What's the story, player?

PONNEY: Cup
Do ya want to take a ponney of milk to bed with ya?

QUEENIE: Man with feminine traits
He's a bit of a queenie that fella.

QUEERHAWK: Strange individual
He's some queerhawk.

RADS: Radiators
Turn on the rads, I'm freezing.

RASA: Raspberry cordial drink
Two pints of rasa and a bag of Taytos please.

RCYC: Snobby yachting person
Schull is always full of rcyc types.

READ: To talk behind someone's back
I heard you were reading me the other night.

RUBBER DOLLIES: Trainers
Dunnes are selling daycent rubber dollies for a tenner.

SCA: Gossip/News
Have ya any sca for me?

SNEDGER: An insulting term meaning someone who sniffs the
bicycle seats of young ladies. A pervert basically
He is a bit of a snedger, that fella.

TO BE FLAHED: To be taken advantage of
You were flahed if you paid 2000 yoyos for that car.

WASH THE WARE/DO THE WARE: To do the washing up
I have to do the ware before I go out.

WAZZIE: Wasp
Mam, I'm after getting stung by a wazzie.

THE SMALLIES

ALLEY ALLEY: Children's game where someone throws a ball behind them and guesses who has caught it.
Alley alley who has the ball,
Is she big or is she small
Is she fat or is she thin
Or is she like a safety pin?

BABA: Child's word for other people

BADINAS: Togs/Swimming costume
Did ya bring yer badinas with ya?

BAREAAHS: Not wearing any shoes or socks
Don't be going on the rocks in your bareaahs.

BEE-BAA: Child's word for an ambulance, police car or fire engine.

BILLY BILLY BAKER: Popular Cork children's rhyme said when making sandcastles. The child taps the upturned bucket with a shovel and recites the following verse:
Billy Billy Baker
Fry a piece of paper
Send him up, send him down
Send him all around the town

BON BONS: Swans
C'mon we go out the Lough to feed the bon bons.

BURN THE BISCUIT: Game where someone hides something and the others have to find it

CHEESER/GRINDER: Getting hit on the ass by a ruler or by the back of someone's hand in school.
Get him and we give him a cheeser.

CHESSIES: Horse chestnuts
We got a rake of chessies down the Bishop's Palace the other day.

CONNIHALY: Penis
I have an awful pain in me connihaly since I got hit with the sliotar.

ECKA: Homework
Nolan gave us a load of ecka so I won't be able to go out tonight.

FAT PIGS: Woodlice
Mam! There's a fat pig in the toilet.

FONDIES: Hugs and kisses
Give yer mam fondies before we head off.

GARY/BURN (2): Go/A chance
Gis a gary of yer new BMX.

GLASSEY ALLEYS: Marbles
I got 2,342 glassey alleys in my collection boy.

GOBS: Game played with small white stones on a beach
C'mon we have a game of gobs.

GRUNDY/UNDY GRUNDY: School torture where you rip
someone's underpants off
Get him down and we give him a grundy.

ICE LOLL: Ice lolly. In most other parts of Ireland, people seem
to say lolly as opposed to loll
If you are a good girl I'll buy ya an ice loll down the shop.

LANGIE: Hanging onto the back of a lorry
I got a great langie yesterday on a Southern Fruit lorry.

LEAVE OFF: To fart
There is some smell in here, who left off?

MERRIES: Amusements
*We went down to the merries in Crosser with the kids last
night.*

NUGGY: Getting hit on the head by someone's knuckles
I've some pain in me head after langerdan gave me a nuggy.

ON THE LANG: Not attending school
Seanie Murph was on the lang yesterday, he spent the day in Top Pool.

PICKEY: Street game like hopskotch
The smallies are always playing pickey.

RAIDING: Stealing from someone else's bonfire pile
We're going raiding off Grattan Street's bona.

RUSSIAN BOOTS: Wellingtons
Put on yer Russian boots if you're going out in the rain.

SEANIE POOLS: Corporation refuse lorries
Johnny Brown drives a seanie pool for the corporation.

SHELLITY HORN: Snail
Stop squishing the shellity horns boy.

SLOGGING (2)/SLOCKING: Stealing apples
We went slogging apples out in a house in Ballinlough the other night.

SMALLIES: Kids
The smallies have challenged us to a game of ball.

STEERNA: Homemade go-cart
I'm looking for four pram wheels to make a daycent steerna.

UP AGAINST THE WALL: Street football game played against a wall
C'mon we have a game of up against the wall.

UP FOR THE BAA: When kids make their confirmation in some schools in the city it is a tradition to buy lots of sweets and throw them out to the other kids in the school who bate the heads off one another to get them. The shout 'up for the baa' goes up when the throwing starts

WE ALL WENT TO YOUGHAL: Popular kids' rhyme
We all went to Youghal
We left the baby fall
My mother came out and gave me a clout
And turned me into a bottle of stout

FOOD

BASKET: Type of bread loaf
Pick up a basket in McCarthy's when you're in town.

BATE/BAAT: Piece of bread/Sandwich
Do ya want a bate with the tea?

BLACKAS: Blackberries
We're going up the back airport road picking blackas later.

BODICE: Ribs
I got a grand bit of bodice down the English Market for the dinner.

CRUBEENS: Pigs' feet. This word is of Irish, not Cork origin, but Cork is one of the few places in Ireland where the word is still in common use.
There is nothing like a good feed of crubeens and a lash of pints.

DONKEY'S GUDGE/CHESTER CAKE: Cake made from the leftovers in a bakery
Gis a bit of yer donkey's gudge.

GOODIE: Traditional Cork dessert made with hot milk, bread and sugar
I love a bit of goodie for supper meself.

MEBS (2): Small potatoes
Make sure the vegetable man doesn't put any mebs in the bag.

POPPIES/POPS: Potatoes
The poppies are very small this year.

SKIRTS AND KIDNEYS: Cheap bits of meat
We're having skirts and kidneys for the dinner today.

SKULL: Type of bread loaf
Pick up a skull and a bottle of milk on your travels.

TRIPE AND DRISHEEN: Cork delicacy comprising of sheep's stomach and pigs' blood. The city was known as drisheen city in the nineteenth century
My nan makes lovely tripe and drisheen.

UCKS: The end of an apple
I bags the ucks.

WIDOW'S MEMORY: Sausage
Gis a bag a chips and a widow's memory.

MONEY FOR NOTHING

BOBS: Money
Have you any bobs on ya?

CONJUN BOX: Savings box
Make sure and put some of your confirmation money away in your conjun box.

DIDDLUM: Type of savings scheme often operated within a company between workers
They are running a diddlum at work to save up for Christmas.

GRADE: Money
I haven't got any grade on me.

MANAGE: Type of savings scheme often run amongst families and friends. Loans can be taken interest free to pay for communions, etc.
If you are passing Lough Road drop in the manage money for me.

SCRIP/SCRIPT: Weekly or monthly subscription fee to club members
Have you got your scrip with you this week?

HANDY ABUSIVE TERMS

FLOG OFF: Go away
Flog off and don't be annoying me.

GONK: Stupid person
He's some gonk that fella.

GOWL: Idiot
Go way ya gowl ya.

HOP OFF: Leave me alone
Hop off now fast I'm telling ya.

LANGBALL: Idiot
He's a right langball.

LANGERDAN: Fool
You're some langerdan, aren't ya?

LATCH: Idiot
This word seems to have gone out of fashion in recent years
G'wan ya latch.

SPADGY: Insulting term meaning idiot
You're some spadgy alright.

OLD CORK SLANG

A TOUCH OF THE HIGOS: Cowardly

AISH: Person

AS OLD AS ATTY HAYES' GOAT: Ancient

AWAY FOR SLATES: Heading for success

BALBHAN: Rude person

BALL IN CAP: Old street game

BALLYHAYS: Mess

BAND HOUSE PLAYER: Bad card player

BANJO: Fight

BANKER: Stonemason's workbench

BAUSEKAWN: Weedy looking person

BAWL OFF: To give out to

BAZER: Punch

BEE UP: Game like pitch and toss

BOLGER: Cranky person

BOSTOON: Fool

BRANNING THE MAYOR: Former custom in Cork of throwing a mixture of bran and water at the newly-conferred Lord Mayor.

BRI: Hill

BRUS (1): Small fragments of a broken object

BRUS (2): Broken sweets

BUCK: Silly conversation

BULL'S EYE DAY: Day for collecting army pension

BUTT: Cart

CABBY HOUSE: Doll's house

CAT AND DOG: Old street game

CAWHAKE: Jinx

CLING: Brawl

CLONAKILTY GOD HELP US: Workhouse

COLLERAH: Noisy scolding woman

CONNY BUN/DODGER: Bread bun eaten during lent

CORONATIONS: English coins

CRACKAWLY: Stupid

CUT A SCATTER: To dress well

DARBY: Small whiskey

DEAD MAN: Man who collected funeral insurance

DECLINE: TB

DOONY DAWNY: Small person

DOUBLE DECKER SHAWL: Superior garment

DRUM: Social meeting of the military

DUST: Stonemason's trade

FAKIN: Fishing illegally with nets

FECK: Game of pitch and toss

FEED THE WAGON: Sporting term meaning to play safe

FOOSTER: Hurry

FOR CHOICER: For free

GATTLE: To chase girls

GAUZER: Good-looking girl

GAZA: Gas lamp

GEANC: Snub nose

GET YOUR GALLON: To be made redundant

GLAUM: To pull someone's hair

GLIMMERMAN: Gasman

GOLLOP: To eat something quickly

GONONSTRIPS: Instructions

GOWRIES: Intelligence

GRIG: To tempt/Tease

GUBBERA: Person who repeats the speech of their elders

GURREY: Homemade go-cart

HAND ME DOWN THE MOON/PAPER THE MOON: Tall person

HARDSHIPPING: Difficult

HATTY ONE: Woman who wears a hat instead of a shawl

HOOFLER: Trickster

HUGGER MUGGER: Whispering

IN A RISHARRIG: Clumsily

JOCKEY: Coin which lands on a jack in a game of feck

JOLLY: Favourite

KNAWVSHAWLING: Finding fault with something

LAW DI DAW: Affected snobby person

LICK ALIKE: Identical

LOP: Old penny

LOSSET: Table used by sellers on the Coal Quay

MAKE: Half penny

MARLY: Lino

MASHER: Good-looking man

MAUZY: Having large hips or heavy buttocks

MAYING: Visiting the countryside on May Sunday

MAYSHAWLER: Clumsy person

MICKEY MACK: Failure/Mess

MOLLY: Apple

MOTION: Desire for sex

MOYLOW: Drunk

NATIONAL: Collection

NOOKS: Money

ODDS: Cakes

OWNSHUCK: Silly, giddy person

PAWNY: Water/Rain

PRE-DOM: Pint bottle of stout

PRIZAWN: Small and scrawny

RED BELLY: Minnow

RIDER: Term used in a game of feck

SCATTER (2): Bandiness

SCUTTLE: To smoke cigarette butts

SHAWLY: Woman who wears a shawl

SHERANG: Foreman

SKALP: To cheat

SLIP THE RING: Pigeon racing term to describe the taking off of the ring on a pigeon's leg after its return from a race. The owner would then run with the ring to a timing clock which was of equal distance from the different lofts

SMUSH: Face

SPAZZY: Pre-decimal sixpence

SPRAT'S EYE: Three penny bit

SPRIGGING: Catching birds

SPUR: Short sighted

SQUIRT: Small addition of stout to give a creamy head on a pint

STRAWKHAULING (2): A reply to the question, how are you? Means struggling along

TARRY BOY: Randy male

TASPY: Good spirited

THRILL: Inclination to buy everyone a drink

THUNDER UP THE GULLEY: Game where kids used to put paper up a drainpipe and light it

TIERCE: Cask and its contents

TULLOCK: Blow to the body

VAMP: To walk

WAMMON: Huge fish

SOME CLASSIC CORK PHRASES

I WILL IN ME AH/EYE/RING: There is no way I'll do that

BELT AWAY: Carry on with what you are doing

THAT WILL SOFTEN HIS COUGH: That will put him in his place

DON'T BE CODDIN' ME: Don't be trying to fool me

CHALK IT DOWN: I agree with you

FAIR DUES/FAIR BOWLS: Well done

GO WAY OU' DAT: You're talking rubbish

HOW'S THE FORM?: How are you?

THE RAIN THAT FELL WAS NO ONE'S BUSINESS: The rain was very heavy

HE NEVER LOST IT: That's typical of him

ME NERVES ARE AT ME: I'm nervous as hell

I HAVEN'T A TOSSER ON ME: I have no money

HE HAS NO MASS ON THAT: He has no respect for that

HOW ARE WE NOW OLD STOCK?: Greeting to a friend

SHUR WHERE WOULD YOU BE GOING: You won't get better than that

THAT FELLA WOULDN'T GIVE YOU THE STEAM OFF HIS PISS: That fella is very mean

I WOULDN'T GIVE HER THE SOOT OF IT: I wouldn't give her the benefit of it

MY HEART IS SCALDED FROM THEM: They constantly harrass me

I'M UP TO NINETY WITH HIM: I worry a lot about him

ALRIGHT BOY: Greeting to a friend

DON'T TAKE A TACK OF NOTICE OF HIM: Don't pay him any attention

I BUST YOUR HEAD FOR YA IF YOU'RE NOT CAREFUL: I'll beat you up if you don't stop annoying me

I'M BATE OUT: I'm exhausted

DID SHE COME ACROSS WITH THE GOODS?: Did you go all the way with her?

I'M BROWNED OFF: I'm fed up

HE DOESN'T DO A TAP: He doesn't do anything

I'M PASSING OUT WITH THE HEAT: The heat is too much for me,

HIS HAIR IS ALL TO ONE SIDE LIKE THE TOWN OF FERMOY: Used when someone has their hair parted to one side

HER POLE MUST BE SOFT: She is not all there

THE ALPHABET OF CORK

BIBLIOGRAPHY

Beecher, Seán, *A Dictionary of Cork Slang* (The Collins Press, Cork, 1996)

Cramer, Tim, *The Life of Other Days* (The Collins Press, Cork, 1992)

Creedon, Cónal, *Pancho and Lefty Ride Out* (The Collins Press, Cork, 1995)

Creedon, Cónal, *Passion Play* (Poolbeg Press, Dublin, 1999)

Cooke, Richard T., *My Home by the Lee: The people's history of Cork* (Irish Millennium Publications, Dublin, 1999)

Crystal, David, *The English Language* (Penguin Books, UK, 1988)

Dolan, Terence P., *A Dictionary of Hiberno-English* (Gill and Macmillan, Dublin, 1999)

Dunne, Seán, *The Cork Anthology* (Cork University Press, 1993)

Lehane, Tadg, *Cork's Own Town: Wise and Otherwise* (Studio, Cork, 1978)

MacCarthy, W.G ., *A Short History of Cork* (Killeen Books, Cork, 1996)

McElligott, Tom, *Six O'Clock All Over Cork* (Wolfhound Press, Dublin, 1992)

McKeon, Jim, *Echoes at the Fountain* (Acorn Press, Cork, 1999)

Murphy, Seamus, *Stone Mad* (Routledge and Kegen Paul Ltd, London, 1966)

Share, Bernard, *Slanguage: A Dictionary of Irish Slang* (Gill and MacMillan, Dublin, 2003)

Svartvik, Jan, *Engelska* (Pan Books, 1999)

Walsh, Enda, *Disco Pigs* and *Sucking Dublin* (Nick Hern Books Ltd, 1997)

OTHER SOURCES

Evening Echo Archive

peoplesrepublicofcork.com

The Archive Newsletter

The *Cork Examiner* Archive

google.com

Websters Online Dictionary